Of Buckwheat and Barley

Jan Coulter

ISBN: 978-81-19654-66-6

First Edition: 2024
Rs. 200/-

Cyberwit.net
HIG 45 Kaushambi Kunj, Kalindipuram
Allahabad - 211011 (U.P.) India
http://www.cyberwit.net
Tel: +(91) 9415091004
E-mail: info@cyberwit.net

Printed at Repro India Limited.

Dedicated to my Brothers

David and Lee

Contents

2 am

Wet as a fish am I, out in
a regular "pea souper,"
opaque as a blanket,
forbidding view.

Bearings all but lost,
shrouded in these arms of fog, which
leave droplets upon my eyelashes and
stroke the earth, still radiating day's warmth.

Led by the waning aura of moon,
her light refracts through puddle and pond,
a setting so familiar, into which we are lost,
among the creaking, of ancient locust tree.

4 am

Looking in from outside, through windows
aglow with amber hue, flickering
wood stove, beckons me, to this
minimal, soft, alluring place.

Spirits play along ceiling beams,
mimicking fire's dance, while outside,
wood smoke encircles the moon and back,
wafting through the very fabric of me.

Stars in great profusion,
reach down to touch the morning.
Coyotes raise their voice in greeting and
rooster cracks the dawn.

Into the gloaming light and warmth,
four legged and I are summoned home,
where shadows still dance in harmony,
with the song of Mother Moon.

4:45 AM

I wish my pencil,
strong of lead,
could dance across a page.

Some moon lit eve,
it does just that,
using stardust for words.

Sliding down on a beam,
through my window, ajar,
a poem is released.

A Contemplation

Poetry is conceived,

when passion commits

to paper,

words which paint an image,

conjuring an emotion,

penetrating the heart.

A Final Summons

For ten years, perhaps twelve,
a sealed envelope held my soul.
Heart's sorrow cried a tapestry, woven with
colours named courage and challenge.

Deep and deeper to the core, a journey.
Dark without light, short on breath, with
air doled out in capillary pockets, resting in
silent repose, where the dead can dance.

And dance they do, words withheld,
gestures, indicate a meeting.
Image brief, message paints care,
brushed with experience.

Learn, these steps of expression, this
language of mute empathy.
Sound penetrates the marrow of spirit.
Touch withheld, embrace in abeyance.

Hands outstretched, pull away.
Pushing against a final summons.
Time will call, promising safety.
It will be nurturing; and you will follow.

Afternoon

At my desk,
window ajar;
suddenly,
a magnificent breeze
graces my cheek,
caresses the very
substance of me;
I breathe deeply.

A Frozen Dawn

Slender, brittle, grasses curl.
Encased in fairy like crystals of ice,
they arch themselves over,
in silent, frozen,
troubled shapes.

Maple's buds,
shiver beneath this
frigid layer.
Branches bend
to this weight of dawn.

A sheen on the land,
coats all; a glistening hue.
May soft breezes warm,
lest vegetation yield, to the
cracking and snapping of limbs.

On this April morn,
I am vexed within,
for their burden
is heavy and
I feel their angst.

A Generous Gesture

Approach tentative.
No wish to intrude.

Your arms open wide,
a grand embrace.

Spontaneity so warm,
a generous gesture.

Acceptance, inclusion,
gratitude.

A Haiku Morning

The cardinal sings.

Spring moves the clouds.

The passerines return.

A Raven's Lament

I grieve inside your grief, edges
raw and heavy and sharp,
searing a hollow within your heart.
A well so deep, sides so slick,
you cannot climb.

My arms extend
toward your anguish.
Your sobbing frame
heaves, near convulsion,
writhing through acute pain.

This place of dark despair,
will claim your soul;
like a liquid pall,
drowning you, binding you,
entwined in this shroud of loss.

Listen to the heartbeat
of dawn, who wakes to
hold you close, within
this lament of grief,
this melody of healing.

Hear forest's song and
raven's cry, for
they will set you free.
Out of darkness;
you shall breathe again.

A Swarming

Did they grow up frightened,
without am open mind?

Were they not nurtured
devoid of the ability to care?

Disregarded, disrespected,
have they learned to hate?

So firmly instilled,
colours the capacity to think.

Careful to sign blame; for
society has flagrantly, misfired.

A Thousand Forests

I could wring out the air,
to quench the thirst, of a
thousand forests
burning.

An event about which, I cannot fully recount.
Searing loss of habitat, destruction of all,
reduced to a cinder,
hot and angry.

The winds are weeping,
tears unable to staunch the rage,
this scorch upon the land, devouring;
even, the path less travelled.

Slowly, the eking out of
moisture from an ashen ceiling.
Rain; a forgotten commodity, precious
quenching, dampening down, to extinguish.

Acknowledgement

So like you am I.
In every feature and facet.
My hands, my frame and
my quiet, gentle, demeanour.

You taught me the beauty
of language.
You taught me to articulate
thought.

I did not excel scholastically, but
I did receive accolades.
In life I became whole,
I became a poet.

Afternoon

At my desk,
window ajar;
suddenly,
a magnificent breeze
graces my cheek,
caresses the very
substance of me;
I breathe deeply.

Alone

When alone,
really alone,
no one is watching
your every vapid move, the

disconnect you feel,
the passing of time,
where guilt clings, to the
measured ticking of thought.

Alone is not void of
construct or confusion;
anxious thought can
fill every molecule.

Alone is chameleon, with
capacity to absorb emotion's
colour, the taste of all seasons,
palate of artists, shades of experience.

Rich and full of peace,
guide this nurturing of soul,
your precious sanctuary;
your alone.

An August Evening

Sultry scorch of July has lifted.
Evenings crisp and clean.
Woodsmoke wafts memories of comfort.

Night stars, beckon to be held, while
crickets raise their voice to Mother Moon;
the nocturnal, are guided by her light.

Eyes wide and wider still, to see
through a darkened way,
under this veil of evening bold.

Drawn am I, to this liminal sanctuary,
where breath is slow, and creatures
leave footprints at river's edge.

Anointing Moons

Snow moon,

hunger moon,

hangs high,

in this dark lure of night.

Light our way,

into dawn,

where possibilities,

are born.

Back Into Self

Desk papers suddenly unhinge,
responding to moon's breath, as
stars purse their lips,
augmenting the breeze.

Some nights are not so easy,
when words struggle and resist the page.
Restless, anxious mind; mistakenly
relives a past event.

Excruciating minutia of detail recalled.
Is the cost of wanting too dear?
Their are no moon beams or star dust,
to ease our landing back, into self.

Only in returning,
do we realise, how far
our boat has travelled,
out, upon the tide.

Balance

Moved by music,
captivated by art,
nurtured with a leaf's passing.

I ache, with life's sorrows,
weep ,with song's melody
smile with coyotes call;

I am complete.

Before the Storm

Dark, ominous ,
cloud thick sky, where
moisture ekes out
upon a land,
so anxious to drink.

Gathering in intensity,
ceiling lowers, as if to
squeeze all creatures out to watch.
Black and blacker still, its
pressure builds to a crescendo.

Silent now, the
spectacle evolves.
Swallow thunder.
Smell lightning.
Listen to the quiet, before the storm.

Black Locust

Moon's light, crisp and clear
guides our way.
Filters, between crag like fingers,
of ancient Locust tree.

Branches reach out,
arthritic hands, bent and twisted, their
palms, an intricate road map
of life's adventures.

Tree trunks, bark deep as fjords,
carved and fissured as a
witch's tale, upon this eerie night,
sentinels of the light, who

tell of strength and capability,
experience and accomplishment,
all embodied in this arbour
of distinction.

Blessed August

Super moon, huge and full,
ascends above south mountain, in
all its warm, orange dress.

Bold, commanding of sky,
she lights our way to dawn.
Fairies of the night,

set up their big top tents of
gossamer, woven between
blades of grass, punctuated by

stocks of wild Mullen,
sporting their fall attire of
burnished brown.

Greens of summer blend in
perfect harmony, with weeds tall,
prolific and abundant.

Oh blessed August,
relief from scorched July,
how favourably, I look upon your demeanour.

Breath of Spring

A single room

with a single bed and

a single chair,

the window spare,

a gossamer curtain

bends in Spring's breath.

Captive

Held by a tether,
that stretches,
but never breaks.

Held within these
deep, dark pockets, where
silence is language.

Held in solitude,
between hurt and longing;
befriend this discomfort.

Held, within a still, shallow,
breath of air.;
captive.

It could have been so beautiful.
It would have been so dangerous.

City Boundary

Buffeted about

by winds that howl,

between tall towers, of

concrete and steel, in a

city that has burst its boundaries,

encroaching upon green spaces,

we were supposed to leave, for

posterity; or was that

prosperity and greed?

Concerto

The first violinist
plucks 'Concert A', and the
melodic cacophony of
instruments, begins to tune.

So it was on my morning walk.
This orchestra, this philharmonic
symphony of spring, utters dulcet vibrations
dancing on the air of dawn.

Thieving blue jays, early warbler and
boreal chickadee,
blend voice with the clatter
of winter's runoff.

Brook sings, between a
chant and a rage,
heading to the river, then beyond,
beyond to the sea.

Water carries these melodies,
an elixir of land and
creatures present. A captive audience are we;
listen to the concerto of spring.

Condensed Into a Moment

Damp, across an exhausted brow,
her wild hair parts.
Dishevelled mind, thinks only of sustenance.

Shoes so thirsty, their tongues pant,
above pavements scorch, while
laces drag through the dust of high noon.

She pushes a battered, stolen, grocery cart,
packed with belongings of necessity.
Its wheels stick and grind under load.

Limping, through a lifetime of
enduring pain, she leans heavily
against the rickety transport.

Evicted from her patch of grass,
a search for shelter;
her tent, as worn and fragile as she is frail.

All earthly trappings,
condensed into a moment, while she
lowers her head and fades from view.

Coral Reef

I was going to 'click' on by,
when I began to wonder,
what this slow moving
show of vibrant colour,
could teach me.

Coral reef,
long ago destroyed;
by us . . . shines for a
brilliant hand with camera, who
made sure we would remember.

I breathe into sea turtle
gracefully ascending,
sea horse hiding and
solitary fish, darting for
cover and safety.

To be this aware,
to stimulate all senses, to
think what is lost.
I could learn again.
I could live slower.

Dance of Time

It was a sweet time
a precious time, a
long time ago.

A time for passion,
for yearning; an
event not forgotten.

I grieve that sweet time,
the dance of time,
a long time ago.

I miss the sweet touch
the gentle touch; I did not know
was empty.

Memories cling , with tight grasp,
not to be repeated; afraid to lose sight . . .
It was a long time ago.

David

October 1937—March 2019

Waves lick at your ashes.
I want to travel with you.
I want to hold you back.

Ebbing with the tide, like
sand between fingers;
I have no rite to detain you.

This journey is pre-ordained,
earthly wishes fulfilled,
place of rest honoured.

I speak as your remains slide away,
"go free, brother, go free.
I will find you, at my passing."

Dawn 'till Dusk

A scant slice of blue sky,
fights off days of dark.
Welcome this haze of sun, which

leaves a yellow grey ceiling, that
leaks through cracks on angel slides,
to greet a chilly morn.

Faces turn upward,
to catch the rays,
of a long with-held warmth.

Branches laugh in a brisk breath
of dawn, usher in our day and
turn a cold shoulder to the

shackles of winter. We
cast off blankets that
insulate our bodies and our minds.

Free are we to leap into spring,
to trip the light fantastic, and
dance from dawn 'till dusk.

Demise of Rose

I wake to a profusion of

rose petals, upon my desk and

notebooks. I am reminded that

beauty in nature is fleeting;

only for those who do not stay,

for the final act.

Dipped in Cloud

Horizontal, hard hitting,
west and north windows.
Hurling splats of rain,
reminiscent of snow,
wet and heavy.

Witness this magic layering.
Striations of hurricane sky,
full of purpose.
A perfect palate of greys,
intensifying to blacks.

In stillness, listen to the
rhythm of your breath.
Time, packaged into a moment,
stretched into a memory,
painted with brush, dipped in cloud.

Energy Inert

Leave me,

abandon me,

allow me to feel.

Now feed me,

nourish my soul;

give me

music,

candlelight and

the night.

Escape

Afraid is the child,
to come out from within
an empty hollow,
where there are tears and quiet fears.

Come the dawn,
drones will cease to fall,
remnants of smoke will clear and
the thunder of tanks will dissipate.

Equilibrium of thought returns,
to a balance of sentiment, no longer
red and searing and hot, but a
cloak of memory.

Exit this void, where the
echo of silence is too loud.
Escape to your core, where breath slows and the
breeze will heal your soul.

Evensong

Coyotes croon and quaver,
splitting the dark with
yipping laughter.

Spring Peepers cantillate,
at decibels extreme and
bull frogs sonorously serenade,

the quiet of moon's rising.
So also must I,
utter notes of welcome,

being privy
at this late hour, to
so many vespers.

Feather Black

Crows, curious.
Excite with objects shining.
Their crack of voice
splits the dawn.

Raven's voice mimics a
wooden spoon in a glass bottle.
A solitary creature, soaring
through the vapours, silently.

Starlings, black, spotted, iridescent,
perform in the hundreds, their aerial
display, a co-ordination, an
aerobatic show of precision.

Stop and wonder, what our
sky would yield, if black birds,
ceased to punctuate our day,
ceased to grace our lives.

Voice mute.
Whir of wing, absent.
Sky vacant.
Species, extinct . . . silence.

Filigree

Moon crisp,

deep into dark sky,

punctuated with cloud.

Ancient locust tree,

fingers interlaced,

a filigree,

resting in night's arms.

Final View

Fabric of life, reveals a journey.

Sticking with glue like substance,

sliding slow as treacle,

becomes our tapestry,

ready to hang on the

walls of our soul, ensuring

our view;

until the end . . .

For a Memory

Sky is rippled like laughing water,
moulding beach sand, undulating,
swirling around my feet.

Pictures invite words,
indelibly, burned
on the C.D. of my mind.

This book of woes slides, as if
upon a slick, slate roof, into consciousness,
within the yearning of thought.

Remember, a sweet gentle sharing,
hold close, this dance of time, the melody, the
music, the rarified air.

Fundy Fog

Stealthily, it slides,
along mountain brow.
Fog of Fundy Bay,
crouching low, seductively creeping,

over hill and hummock, as an
antique quilt would
slide off a foot board, itself in repose.
This haze of vapour, slick as oil,

viscous as molasses, forms a
heavy blanket, which folds itself, into the
landscape, its fringe of fingers touch
every rock and tree alike; but, the

sun will rise,
earth's pallor will lift, as
currents of warmth, burn off this
valley brume, this shroud of Fundy Fog.

Gates

Old gates, which stand alone,
with no attachment
to fences, or
anything at all, rest

quietly in their solitude.
They stand to invite,
to welcome and beckon
passers by, to enter this

opportunity,
this wooden gate.
Held between uprights,
latched to posts, with

rusted iron hinges,
forged long ago. The
tang slips into its catch; a
positive metallic click; closed.

And so it stands alone, waiting
for the next guest to enter,
to great a chance encounter
with no attachment
to anything at all.

Held In A Moment

Wild roses three, the
colour of their name,
defend with thorns,
sharp and plentiful.

Rain drops rest heavily
upon petals, shielding
pollen rich stamens,
their anther and filament too.

Buds, pert and upright
are soon to blossom, while
a surprised spider takes up
residence, within my view.

How special the magic,
drink in all the stages,
witness these vignettes of beauty,
held in a moment of time.

Homage

They have passed on , our elders.
Vibrant contributors
to a community,
richer for their presence.

Ancestors moulded and shaped
this landscape, this valley; a
bucolic mosaic, woven with
honour and gratitude.

Now, part of this
older generation, I come here
prepared, my tenure, a mere
thirty-four years, yet I am

steward of my land,
holding this valley sacred, as
I write about her beauty and
give homage to those gone before.

In Passing

Even in death, leaf's
veins protrude,
like bones of a body.
Flesh between ribs
wanes and shrivels.

Soft green, now faded
yellow ocher, will whither,
to a gentle brindle, where
edges curl and retreat, as
stem crooks in a passive fairwell.

I wonder—-
how such beauty is
allowed to pass; and I marvel
at how much beauty, there is
in passing.

In The Distance

Sunrise of red and orange,
mimics a stunning sunset.
Vermilion streaks, swim between rivers of sky,
punctuated with cloud like lakes.

Awakening sun, pushes my vignette upward,
out from this drawer of night.
Light bends, through the haze of cold,
greeting an adventure, about to be warmed.

So quickly changes this composition.
Streaks of vivid, red like orange, now a bold hard light,
celebrating this dawn,
illuminating valley, hill and dale.

Tempt the artist of our morning,
to capture, what seems a sweet mirage.
All is quiet, while in the distance,
a lone dog barks.

Inheritance

Rage hangs in a
precarious balance,
between guilt and
obligation.

Self esteem, lost.
Shoved deep in a drawer,
along with trust and
expectation.

Come into this day,
look hard at the origin of
fear and rejection; an
element of the past.

Yesterday's smothered
spirit; your essence,
snuffed out, like a candle
burning low.

Your light diminished, ebbing
away, all that I have
known you to be; your soul,
but a burning ember.

Into the Still

Thoughts mellow; echo
between sound and sight.
A restful, peaceful state of being.

Folding day over into evening,
darkness slides into valley,
radiating day's warmth.

Spring Peepers break any notion of silence,
celebrating the recent rain with song—-a
signature of spring's cold ending.

Breezes soft, rustle as
air wafts redolent of fresh mown grass;
so rich, so pungent, tongue tastes.

Time neither waxes or wanes,
appearing to stand still,
inviting us, to do the sane.

Magic

Sawdust languishes
on soft sun beams, which
stream into my shop, to
grace this gentle, May afternoon.

Shavings vibrate atop whirring tools, which
shake themselves into intricate
patterns of art and I picture sand,
raked into creative order.

Smell the intoxicating aroma,
lumber's scent, intensified,
by milling out
this precious stock.

Time has passed.
Perhaps; my last commission,
I cannot imagine, as a
hue of magic lingers.

Tools off,
shop at rest, silence; as
soft sun streams . . .
Yes,
magic.

Market Morning

As I drive,
shadows long,
lick pavement, as
morning sun,
strobes through
skeletal trees, in
rapid,
metronome,
rhythm.

Memories and Pictures

For Michelle

Shadows chase my mind in turmoil.
Generous is time, rich in content, but,
will I run empty, before the void?

Regret shall not plague me.
Life, well sampled,
years kind in that regard.

Perhaps sorrow; not tasting the dawn, or
holding stars with Mother Moon,
will sadden my heart, but,

I have made memories with pictures,
to nurture my path.
I shall not want, but for that

knowing look, a kind embrace,
the gift of laughter and
your gentle smile.

Memory Within

Memory is
an illusive commodity.
Curious, how the mind,
selectively
reorganizes,

time and events.
Painful moments,
crisp and taut,
visit thought,
frequently.

Locked inside a
boundary, we
protect the heart,
from flagellation
of the mind.

We are bold, we are
courageous. We have
nurtured well;
our memory within.

Mere Mortals

A quiet moon sets the stage,

for an evening of muted light.

Her veiled aura is accompanied with

stars so numerous;

I don't believe,

they wished to be counted.

A galaxy of burning embers, are

souls travelling onward, not

joined, by we mere mortals.

Mirage

Ankle deep in summers dress,
leaves rain around me.
My boots swish through.
I want to pick up all colours, and
press between waxed papers, to keep.

A solitary row of trees, erect and tall,
sing a forest's memory. A mirage,
false as a lie, which fails to hide,
vicious clear cuts, obliterating an era of respect.
Hold tight this fleeting memory.

Deer and coyote; gone, dispersed.
Bird song; all but disappeared.
May flower and fern; deleted.
How selfish to destroy,
even the whisper of regrowth.

Mistaken

The palms of my hands,
hold a record of
life's experience.
They've not been old 'till now.
They do not know,
what changes are yet to visit.

All the pits and valleys
of despair,
all the summits and crests
of elation,
creases deep as the
journey is profound,

are carved indelibly as a
roadmap, complete with
foot paths.
Flesh and nerve accept this
travel, through callous,
scrape and scar.

There is a reality to face.
This process will not
yield to wish or folly.
Life continued cannot
arrest this change;
but surely . . . the mirror is mistaken.

Moonshine and Moss

Cool night rests on the
tail of a warm day, where
lone coyote sings a
plaintive refrain, over and
over, to welcome the dawn.

To greet the morn with a
crowing kiss, rooster
sounds into the still dark
air, that swells with Spring
Peepers' call.

I seek the liminal places that
nurture and welcome with
generous breath, offering a
calm that draws you in and
may not let you go.

Leafy greens paint valley and mountain
with sable brush, dipped in
moonshine and moss.
Come, drink in the calm and taste this
day of grace; welcome the dawn.

Night Travel

There is a bend
in the light.
It cannot reach me.
Slipping out of cloud
on angel slides from
sun and moon,
stars travel earth bound
teasing my eyes. A
welcome landing, to
blend with the flicker
of firefly.

Of Buckwheat and Barley

For David 1937 - 2019

Smoke ascends from a
hot glowing tip,
resting in a
ubiquitous restaurant
ashtray.

A tailored lamp,
square of base,
shade a deep yellow
ocher, sits upon
a large writing desk.

A plume of smoke, rises like a
delinquent child,
errant and forgotten,
in the playground of
life lingering.

The ash of evening
holds a vision, I struggle to
retain. Time passes, I have
memory fading, into this
whorl of thought.

I cannot remember
your voice, you have
not been gone long.
Your image blurs.
I cannot feel your gaze.

Fingers stretch
through this fog, to
touch my hand; I am not
surprised at how
similar, we have become.

Time fades, I am older now.
You in fields afar,
climbing the fence, come to me, to
show me the difference
between buckwheat and barley.

Of Cloud

Darkness settles, shroud of
haze, blankets valley floor,
coats roof of mouth,
collects stiffly in joints.

Fog, thick and viscous,
licks lip of mountain,
trickling down into pockets deep
and fissures wide, while

steaming vapours rise from
pavement, obliterating view.
Blinded by my light, deer stands
porcupine lumbers,

between asphalt and vapours.
Heavy, this cool crisp air.
Breath labours, nostrils flare.
Inhale the beauty, in these whiffs of cloud.

Of The In Between

Snow,
sticks to spruce fronds,
'make up' of the wild,
dressed for spring's debut.

There is a lull in
this season, a
winter's kiss goodbye;
then the thaw ensues.

Pond ice fractures.
Reflects sky of grey and
echos, the honking
arrival of geese,

who land to rest,
confusing domestic stock.
Perhaps it is envy
of their wild.

A precious interlude
of the in between, leaves us
restless for warmer climes,
anxious for spring's break.

It is the in between,
which nurtures our land,
comforts our soul, and holds
us in awe, from season to season.

Our Demise

Night stars rend the
moon in two,
with ragged
sword of experience.

Her edges raw and
sharp are bleeding
a sad melody; a
refrain I have known.

Yet her beauty sings
through, her light,
barely dimmed by
her sorrow, which leaks

from wounds, of
rape and plunder, of our
land, for profit, for greed;
for our demise.

Perfect Joy

A gossamer veil, hangs
over moon, in an atmosphere,
diffused by a golden aura,
surrounding the muted orb.

One night before 'full', a
Super Moon shows her
handsome face, twice, in this
summer's month waning.

I expect a rumpus, a
congregation of all that's wild, to
trip the light fantastic, to
revel in perfect joy, lasting into dawn.

Poignant Silence

There is a deep pain, within a
desolate hollow, where a
heart once lived,

before it was given away,
without words to describe,
either presence or absence.

Words such as void,
cavernous, bare.
Emptiness sticks to the senses.

Smell of rose turned to musk.
Taste neither sweet nor savoury, but
acrid, caustic, burning.

Hear the echo of
poignant silence as it
throbs inside,

aching chest walls, where
ribs expand and contract,
against a vast vacancy . . .

Perhaps, my heart will be returned,
to my time weary soul.
Perhaps, I shall befriend this quiet,

Perhaps, there is peace within this silence.

Premonition

I had a premonition,
that I would be leaving,
before you.

I'm sure there is a waiting room,
where I may spend thought and
pause, for your arrival.

Give me notebook and pencil,
people to watch,
vignettes to capture; then,

I'll not notice the passing of time,
a concept I have yet to grasp.
Time, a commodity of the present, which

won't be lost or missed.
Absorbed into the past,
woven into an eternity.

Psalm of Gratitude

For so long, a drought. Now, a
forgotten song, the melody of rain.
Land, like creature, drinks. Will it suffice?
Will it quench a thirst so enduring?

There is no growth, not even a weed.
Left to themselves are dandelion stems,
their down like parachutes,
long carried away.

Smell this earth, sweet and dark.
In its solemnity, a dour
graveyard of death, now
whispering relief.

Each stem arched and bent toward
Mother Earth, gradually finds strength,
to stand nourished,
regaining stasis, in this

demanding cycle; or is that circle—
of thirst and sated comfort.
Witness rebirth and utter
psalms of gratitude. May the rains come again.

Raven Wild

For Michelle

Time,
carries lines,
around a smile. An
hourglass, sifts memories
for a soul.

Regret hangs on the edge of an
amend, spoken into a void,
hollow as the breath, that
stretches a heart.

Recollection,
sings a minor
melody, while the
sweet sounds of time
are running out.

Open arms have set you free.
Spread your wings, take the
road less travelled.
Run with raven,
run, with her wild.

Reality

Gone,
into a silence,
I cannot penetrate.

You did not say goodbye.
Your essence lingers
in my heart and I yearn

to reach out, to connect. But,
it is not my place or time.
Now is when I wrap my arms

securely around my
expectations and I bow
to the reality of the day..

Remember

“Please don’t snap the
snapdragons.
It hurts” said you to me.

Now, 65 years on,
you don’t remember.
I, cannot forget.

Remnants

Moon sings
sun and stars
dance, between
ominous cloud.
Thunder roars and
lightening burns,
leaving charcoal
remnants
of the heart.

River Dance

I find dance, in the
choreography of river.
Essential, sacred to many.
Ignored by most.

Canoe sways to water's song,
lapping at bow. I discover
freedom on river wide, paddling to
the rhythm, of my breath.

Merganser, kingfisher and loon alike,
join this orchestra of the wild.
River of dance, sings a melody;
the ballet is about to begin.

Rotten Apples / Wet Wood

Landscape, grey as ash.

Spring's wet cold disposition, a

gardener's disappointment,

farmer's devastation,

apple harvest, a disaster.

Wood cut late,

green smouldering log and

winter is on her way!

Run With the Wild

Tovish (2012–2023)

Poignant, is this loss,
rattling within the boundary of my ribs, with
chest so tight, there is not breath.

Memories collect in the sentiment of grief.
Tears, stain my cheek, as I recall, a
reservoir of images.

Time passes quietly.
Light reflects through this blur of sorrow,
your gaze, your trust, my soul.

Run with the wind, run with the wild,
go free, rest in splendour, while still;
I look to fill your water bowl . . .

Season of Glory

Golden rod bends, from
full measure of height,
down to Mother Earth.

Poplar leaves quiver, while
boughs of silver maple,
nod and dance with grace.

Upon this plume of breeze,
astride as horsemen, ride the
fragrances of fall. Waft of wood smoke,

essence of oak and beech, and the
aroma of crackling pine.
The warmth of fall, settles in.

Soon to return to her skeletal armature,
summer's dress rains around me,
enhancing, this season of glory.

Serious Concern

Shiny, soot black,
tinged with sepia tones,
highlighted with silver sheen;
a crow's feather.

Presenting itself before me,
amid gravel and sand,
I worry that it is lost. I worry
who and where the owner might be.

I, of course, expect a notice
in the Avian Gazette,
announcing a theft, a robbery,
an altercation, resulting in this

careless disregard, of an appendage so vital.
I also worry that sheep,
will shrink in the rain.
Serious concern for a curious 8 yr. old, going on 74!

Shelter

I lean,
into the forest.
She bends
toward me,
folding her arms,
fashioning a
canopy above;
shelter, from the
icy breath that
pierces ribs, the
mockery of
sleet; neither
snow nor rain,
dancing, stinging,
my eyes, my cheeks,
my heart.

Slow Day

Day of grey,
day of rest, follows
heavy deluge, where the
heavens release their urgent song.

Grasses turn inside out,
thin shoulders bent,
coloured silver, in
reflection of day's canvas.

Soft as lambs ears, a
pewter sheen dresses
every branch, twig and trunk of tree.
Air, rich and redolent of earth tones,

a watercolour palate, with
greens soft, yet vibrant,
enhanced in this mist, as
spruce fronds extend their fingers.

A Guernsey cow, led along
an abandoned rail bed, completes this
bucolic event, slow in motion,
as is our day.

Spent

4 am.
I am spent.
Writing exhausted.

Stairs present effort,
an old woman
assumes my frame.

No longer do I chastise
my limbs less respondent.
Quiet gratitude prevails.

Rest ensues, as rooster
hails the dawn and morning dove
coos her gentle greeting.

Good morning.

Summer 1965 —- Musings at 15

She who loves,

loves not only a subject,

but the idea of that emotion.

Until she realises this,

her love will be egotistical.

Tapers of the Night

Dark thought runs wild, with
light and shadow, of night's
bee's wax tapers.

Flame forms stalagmites, rising from
liquid pools, where flows an appliqué,
wax upon wax, dripping, as if

mediaeval, to grace an alter, a
cold, dank castle or haunted
vacant dwelling.

On a wind swept, wind howled, eerie eve,
where witches rule supreme and
crows, her minions, keep the order,

trees bend with moon's exhale and leave
dark thought to run wild, with
light and shadow; tapers of the night.

The Dance of Art

Cord of muscle, sinew long,
stands firm on bronzed frame.
A ripple of movement, smooth and lean,
gestures toward task at hand.

Fingers conduct a symphony.
Forearm glistens
under scorch of
July's summer; unrelenting.

With deft precision,
mortise holds tenon,
spline locks cap and
anchors fasten to wall.

Witness a choreography at play.
Adept, agile, bend and flow,
immersed in creation,
the dance of art.

The Era of Steam

(for Lee)

Coal scuttle,
tender car,
rusted metal,
round headed rivets.

Smell of iron,
heavy taste,
oil and grease,
massive couplers,

reaching like hands,
toward one another.
Familiar the sound, a
connection of precision.

On rusted side rail,
sits roundhouse of the past,
solitary in memory, an
era of industry, an era of shipping.

These were working trains,
of transport and commerce,
boxcar, tanker,
gondola and caboose.

Queen of the yard,
iron, black as death,
steam labourer of old,
grandeur in repose.

Her engine wheels, upon rails,
in numbered sequence,
from front to back,
are grouped in pairs.

Such massive beauty,
from a time now passed,
awaits the connoisseur, of
the era of steam.

The Gift

I struggle
to put words
on a page,

and then;
what binds
graphite to paper—

a gift.
Grateful am I
beyond all measure.

The Lesson

Who stands in the
light of moon,
among the pathway of stars?

Are we born of this
radiance, or have we
to learn its respect, this

energy within, this
heat burning,
never to dull?

These souls, born of the dark,
have not yet
learned to breathe.

May we stand in this light together.
May we teach one another, to
honour and love, without judgement.

The Silence of Night

Peepers cease their evening canticle,
replaced by sonorous bull frog.
Coyotes gather to yip and howl a serenade,
as evening travels under light of moon.

Resounding within this silence,
night voices bounce off hill and vale,
reverberating in the marrow of my bones,
pulling my heart into receptive order.

My night is just beginning.
It is freedom, it is expression,
with all its dulcet tones;
this sacred silence of the night.

T

The Waiting Room

Dog of mine, leaves such a void.
Absence travels beyond grief.
I mourn your presence; gone.

With an ache in the throat,
tears leak from the corners of my heart,
loss makes itself known.

The waiting room speaks in silence,
words gestured, "we are so sorry".
Yes . . . as am I.

The Wee Hours

Why I wonder,
do we say,
“Wee Hours of the Morning?”

They are not in the least ‘wee’ but
full to over flowing,
engaging all the senses.

Teasing palate and eardrum,
pupil and nostril;
rain, precious rain, falls to

pungent earth, redolent of iron,
cool upon the tongue,
dancing with wild abandon.

Hold this sweetness, bring to your lips,
taste its nectar, elixir of the dark and
guest of dawn.

It is here where I write,
It is here where I feel.
It is here where I am whole,

within “the wee hours” of the morning . . .

Time Captured

Sweet spring blooms
into sultry summer,
where images of fall, in
all her glory, pass on,
to the barricades of winter.

Frost sets upon a furrowed brow,
twigs snap under boot, and soon,
snow will sift, into crevices of
heart and soul, where time passes,
before our very breath.

It is this time,
we must capture.
She will escape without notice.
Years of content will pass;
for which we have no memory . . .

Time Escapes

A commodity, illusive, precious,
easily frittered away.
Grip fails,
against force of will.
Time, it slips from grasp.

What seems lost,
merely transferred.
Locked into petal of rose,
eye of dog and
ancient locust tree.

Not always present,
always absorbed.
Thought, deep and focused,
rarely squandered,
yet time, escapes in silence.

To Know

I spent some time
with your books today.

I felt your heart
beating in my chest.

To know someone, is perhaps to
devour that which they write.

To Seed

Thousands upon thousands of
tiny silken parachutes,
carry the germ of springs to follow.
Bend and swirl on

breath of Mother Earth;
a pas de deux, with sun supreme.
Her golden warmth, lifts you, to
dance over swaying Timothy Hay.

Tiny barbs catch a mooring,
travel side saddle on fox's bronzed body,
or grace yielding field and furrow alike,
planting themselves in the smallest declivity.

A profusion,
backlit with gossamer garment,
diaphanous, sheer, shimmering beauty—
The dandelion goes to seed.

Touch

I did not
know,
until I
touched
that emotion,
how raw,
how hot.

How it sears,
the very
core of
my being,
lifted up,
into an ache, that
will not dissipate.

Step closer,
into the angst.
Touch again, that
raw, hot,
emotion,
lodged in the memory,
of every nerve ending.

Know it well,
this lesson, it
will teach you
grace and
patience.
It will,
set you free.

Tree Swallow

Return to me,
familiar
liquid chortle.
Fill the air,
soar high,
into a cerulean sky,
to swoop downward
at warp speed,
to soar again,
upward —-
pure exquisit joy!

War

Buildings tall, bombed and burning,
flames like daggers,
stab the walls, lick her wounds,
yet, she bleeds.

Below this agony, shoe deep in ash,
a solitary child swings,
on a red and yellow swing set, oblivious
to the destruction, the desolate, the damned.

Plumes of smoke, black as ink,
exhale in deadly coughs, into
the sky, the day, the death toll, the dark; and
a red and yellow swing set.

We Are of Ash

Hangs heavy, this quiet inertia.
Robs the soul of purpose,
robs the spirit too.

Apathetic mind, speaks of dormant emotion,
reminiscent of the past, an insurrection of
words against reason and intellect.

Individuals with laboured speech, leave
sensitivities, raw and angular,
carved deep, within a chest that aches.

We are of ragged edge,
dancing bare foot upon the coals of
careless disregard.

We look to Mother Earth,
this fecund soil, into which
we plunge our hands, to root.

Within this nurturing medium,
we will ascend,
out of the fire of memories tether.

We smudge ourselves.
We are of ash.
We are phoenix.

Web of Thought

The dusk spits out fractions
of words, which speak
the night into dark.

Hieroglyphics, etched in the
caverns of the mind,
struggle to find place,

upon the page of reality.
Lured from the web of thought,
anxious suspended syllables

search for exit, from the
contradiction of reason,
arguing with intellect, while

whole sentences play and languish,
waiting for release from mind to page, where
creativity is born of the night.

www.ingramcontent.com/pod-product-compliance
Ingram Content Group UK Ltd.
Pitfield, Milton Keynes, MK11 3LW, UK
UKHW041315190726
13845UKWH00025B/280

9 788119 654666